P9-DNY-780

Ice Breaker

How Mabel Fairbanks Changed Figure Skating

Rose Viña

illustrated by
Claire Almon

Albert Whitman & Company
Chicago, Illinois

Winter nights,
cold and dark,
are no place
for a child.

Yet Mabel sleeps
on an icy stoop
in New York City.
With nowhere to live
and nowhere to go,
she's all on her own.

One day, a woman
spots Mabel
and offers her shelter.
Mabel accepts, and in exchange,
helps babysit the woman's child.

Inside her new home,
Mabel loves to look out the apartment windows
at the park below.
It's a winter wonderland
filled with ice skaters,
jumping and twirling
right into her heart.

Eager to join,
Mabel saves up her money
and buys a pair
of used black ice skates.
But they're two sizes too big.

Mabel won't let that stop her.
She stuffs the front
of the old skates
with cotton wool
and laces them up tight.

As Mabel steps onto the frozen lake,
she glides across the smooth ice
and finds that here,
she belongs.

All winter long
she practices
spins,
spirals,
swizzles.

The more Mabel learns,
the more she wants
to perform in shows,
and become a star.

As the seasons change,
Mabel's frozen haven
slowly melts away.

But Mabel won't let that stop her.
She dashes to the nearest ice rink,
on West 52nd Street.

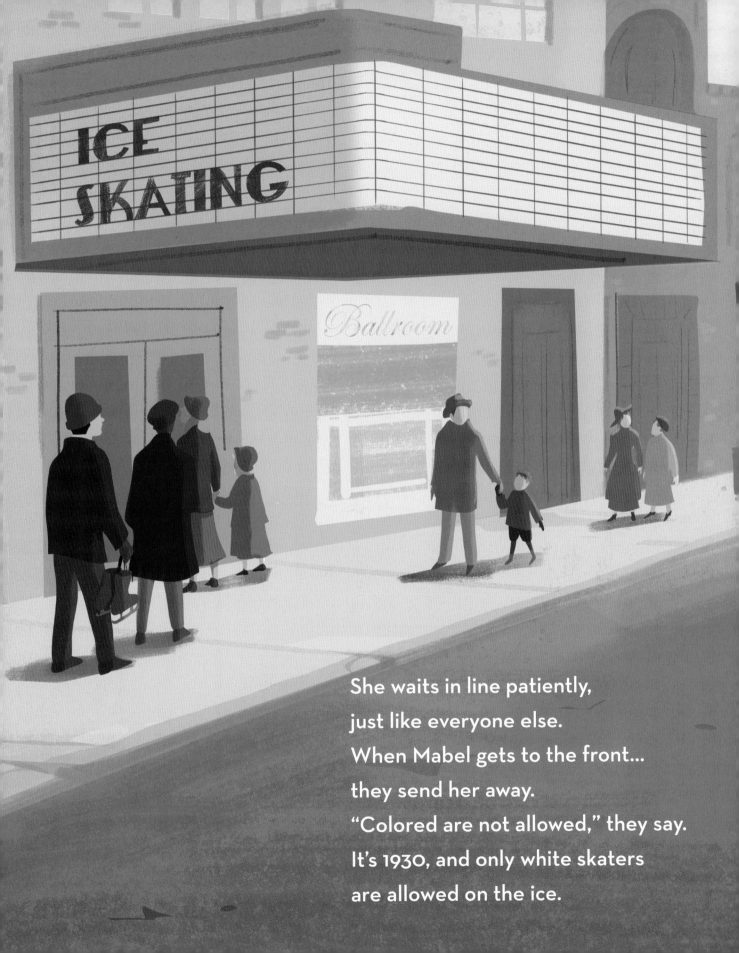

She waits in line patiently,
just like everyone else.
When Mabel gets to the front...
they send her away.
"Colored are not allowed," they say.
It's 1930, and only white skaters
are allowed on the ice.

But Mabel won't let that stop her.
Every day, she returns
to the rink...

and every day,
she is turned away.

Until one evening
a rink manager
lets her in.
"You can skate,
but only when the white skaters
are done training."

Mabel's love
for skating grows
with every jump,
and every fumble.
Mabel enjoys
learning new tricks
as she pushes herself
across the ice,
fast and powerful.

At the rink,
top coaches
see Mabel's talent
and nurture it.
Howard Nicholson
teaches her the lutz jump,
and Maribel Vinson helps her
perfect the layback spin.

Her coaches risk their reputations
for teaching a black child.
They continue to teach Mabel anyway.

Mabel wants to compete for gold medals.

She imagines the world's biggest stage...the Olympics.

To enter competitions, she must belong

to a skating club and pass tests.

But the clubs' officials tell her no.

"Colored are not allowed in skating clubs."

"Colored are not allowed to take skating tests."

But Mabel won't let that stop her.
She wants to join an ice show.

An entertainment manager named Wally Hunter
sees magic in Mabel's skating skills.
He builds a six-foot-by-six-foot
ice tank in her home.
This way she can practice
anytime her heart desires.

Soon Mabel gets skating gigs in Harlem nightclubs.
She delights the audiences
with her sit spin,
split jump,
and spectacular smile.

Mabel likes to stand out when she's on the ice.
She paints her skates pink
and wears flashy, colorful costumes
that shine bright under the spotlights.

Hollywood is looking for ice skaters to perform on the television show *Frosty Frolics*. Mabel packs her bags.

The television show is a hit!
Mabel finds even more success
performing for live audiences in Cuba and Mexico.
But no matter how well she performs,
they still won't let her have star billing,
because of the color of her skin.

Mabel says yes
while the world says no.

But Mabel won't let that stop her.
She hopes that someday
the world will accept
black skaters
on the ice.

She decides
the best way
to make change happen
is to start coaching.

Mabel encourages her students
to work hard and never give up,
no matter how hard they fall
or how difficult the journey may be.

If her students don't have enough money
for skating, Mabel helps.
She buys them their first pair of skates
and admission to the rink.

She teaches them

to leap far,

to spin fast,

to believe.

Mabel demands change
and a path
toward a brighter future.
She commands the Los Angeles Figure Skating Club
to admit her skaters.

Mabel pushes the judges to be fair
to all her students, no matter what they look like.

Now all skaters can join skating clubs,
compete,
and chase their dreams.

Because of Mabel's strong voice
and helping heart,
the icy barriers
were shattered.

About Mabel Fairbanks

Mabel Fairbanks overcame racial barriers to become a pioneer in the skating world and a champion for skaters of color. Of African American and Seminole descent, Mabel was born in the Florida Everglades on November 14, 1915. Orphaned at eight years old, Mabel went to New York City to live with her brother, but the living arrangement didn't work out. At the age of nine she found herself homeless, then fostered by a white family, and soon after, she tried figure skating for the first time.

By the time she was a teenager, Mabel had caught the attention of top coaches and begun mastering many skating skills, including difficult jumps and spins with unique positions. Off the ice, Mabel studied her favorite skaters on television and film. But because of the color of her skin, Mabel wasn't allowed to join any skating clubs—organizations that train and test skaters—which kept her from pursuing figure skating as a competitive sport. Instead, Mabel tried out for Ice Follies, the touring ice show company, and was accepted. She performed internationally through the 1940s but was never offered the role of a principal star, though she was as talented as the white skaters who had star billing.

In the 1950s and 1960s, Mabel turned to coaching. Leslie Robinson, one of Mabel's students, remembers Mabel's influence in shaping his career: "Each year she took her students to the Ice Capades. There were no black skaters in the show until 1966, when they hired some for the chorus. But she knew something was about to break. She got me an audition." Mabel sensed that social change was coming and pushed the skaters of color that she coached to try for starring roles. At the same time, she pressured the Los Angeles Figure Skating Club to start admitting black skaters. With Mabel's coaching, in 1965 Atoy Wilson became the first black man to compete at the US Figure Skating Championships, and in 1966 he was the first black skater to be crowned champion.

Mabel mentored and helped develop the talents of many young figure skaters who went on to become national, world, and Olympic champions, including Kristi Yamaguchi, Tiffany Chin, Debi Thomas, Tai Babilonia, and Randy Gardner. Mabel believed with all her heart that anyone should be allowed to skate, and went to great lengths for skaters who lived in poverty, giving them free skating lessons and buying their first pairs of figure skates. Mabel continued to coach until she reached the age of 79.

In 1997, her efforts were finally recognized, when she became the first African American inducted into the US Figure Skating Hall of Fame. Shortly after she passed away in 2001, she was inducted into the International Women's Sports Hall of Fame for her contributions to coaching.

She is buried at the Hollywood Forever Cemetery, where her gravestone says, "Skatingly Yours."

Glossary of Figure Skating Terms

layback spin While spinning on one foot, the skater arches backward, lowering the shoulders and head toward the ice.

lutz A jump in which the skater uses the toe-pick of the ice skate to launch into the air from a backward outside edge.

sit spin While spinning on one foot, the skater bends the knee to a sitting position while the free leg stretches forward.

spirals While gliding on one foot and maintaining a smooth edge, the skater lifts the other leg as high as possible.

split jump A jump in which the skater achieves a split position in the air.

swizzles A beginner skill in which the skater glides on two feet, smoothly moving the feet outward and inward in an oval shape.

Selected Sources

"International Women's Sports Hall of Fame." Women's Sports Foundation, accessed November 16, 2018. https://www.womenssportsfoundation.org/programs/awards/international-womens-sports-hall-fame/.

Levine, Bettijane. "The Ice Mother Blazed the Skating Trail for Others." *Los Angeles Times*, February 19, 1998. Accessed November 16, 2018. https://www.latimes.com/archives/la-xpm-1998-feb-19-ls-20524-story.html.

"Mabel Fairbanks Harassed by Jim Crow." *The Afro American* (Baltimore). May 5, 1945.

Quintanilla, Michael. "Obituaries: Mabel Fairbanks, 85; Black Ice Skater." *Los Angeles Times*, October 4, 2001. Accessed November 16, 2018. http://articles.latimes.com/2001/oct/04/local/me-53367.

Reed, Christopher. "Obituary: Mabel Fairbanks." *The Guardian*, October 8, 2001. Accessed November 16, 2018. https://www.theguardian.com/news/2001/oct/08/guardianobituaries.

Scheurer, Ronald A. "Breaking the Ice: The Mabel Fairbanks Story." *American Visions*, December 1, 1997.

To my parents, sisters, nieces, nephews, husband,
and "skating family," with love—RV

For all those little girls who keep saying "yes" to their
dreams when others tell them "no"—CA

Library of Congress Cataloging-in-Publication data is on file with the publisher.

Text copyright © 2019 by Rose Viña
Illustrations copyright © 2019 by Albert Whitman & Company
Illustrations by Claire Almon
First published in the United States of America
in 2019 by Albert Whitman & Company
ISBN 978-0-8075-3496-0 (hardcover)
ISBN 978-0-8075-3497-7 (ebook)

Printed in China
10 9 8 7 6 5 4 3 2 1 HH 24 23 22 21 20 19

Design by Morgan Beck

For more information about Albert Whitman & Company,
visit our website at www.albertwhitman.com.

100 Years of Albert Whitman & Company
Celebrate with us in 2019!